INDIAN SOCIETY AND GLOBALISATION

SHWETA DUBEY

Made with ♥ on the Notion Press Platform
www.notionpress.com

"In the honour of my Maa, who showed me how to be a good person by her example every day."

Contents

Foreword

Before going into the details of the Social life and Institutions it will be necessary to keep in mind that India is not a country of any monolithic tradition and there are a variety of religious, ethnic, regional cultural traditions which make this country a land of unity in diversity. Even the Hindus who form the majority of Indian population maintain a number of regional social and cultural patterns along with their languages. It reflects in their organizational hierarchies, practices of marriage, kinship system, status of woman etc. Similarly, each of the major religious communities has its social peculiarities and some variety of social practices.

Yet, there is some common social approach of all the Indian communities with regard to their social behaviour in public and their mutual interactions and inter-communal relations. It is the result of a continuous phenomenon of synthesis between different cultural communities over the centuries of co-existence and co-patriotic progress of the Indian people in the modern age. It is again a manifestation of the attitudes and outlook of the people of this land towards oneself and others including non-human animal world and the nature as a whole which we specifically call Indian.

There are a number of social practices and rituals which the people of this land seem to observe individually or privately implying their concern for the whole humanity and the nature termed as 'jeeva' and 'jagat'. Many of these rites also imply social interactions with persons of different strata and communities. Some of the sacraments are observed exclusively to maintain particular family and cultural tradition. On the other hand, you can see the inter-communal greetings and meetings at the time of religious festivals of one-another community. There are a number of occasions when people use to assemble and interact. These may be of both secular and religious nature. While the religious assemblages are mostly the part of the age-old religio-cultural traditions of India, so many old and new outlets of social gatherings have developed over the ages like musical concerts, theatres, cinemas, sports'-events etc. which speak for the social life of the peoples in this land.

As far as the social institutions are concerned we will have to look into it as per each major religious community which has its own system of social classes and hierarchy, marriage and family customs, kinship bonds etc. The Hindus in particular have a complex social structure based on caste-system and in spite of the modern secular ethos the inter-caste and intra-caste relations become a curious subject of observation. The practice of marriage within one's own caste is a corollary to the caste system of the Hindus. There are a variety of other regional and tribal social institutions also which have to be taken into account for their peculiar systems and practices.

The Hindu view of life is closely associated with the nature and environment. Hindus consider the rivers as their source of life and call them mother. Worshipping everything living or non-living, trees/vegetation, rivers, ponds and mountains and relating a number of birds, animals and even fish to certain godly entities or gods/goddesses speaks volume about this trait of Hindus. This is further extended to the ethos of non-violence and vegetarianism in a large Hindu community. Then the ethics of personal and social hygiene should also be not taken sight of. Thus, a Hindu is always supposed to be concerned with his personal conduct and social obligations both overtly or covertly.

However, a tourist or a stranger should not be made to confuse that all these ideals and ethics are thoroughly observed or practiced by all the Hindus of present day Indian society. A lot of elasticity and flexibility in actual practices is also granted and so many relaxations are recommended in the scriptures itself that there is sufficient scope of deviating from an ideal position. One may undoubtedly find some adherents of the scriptural dictates in the strictly traditional families, in smaller cities and countryside, isolated pockets in hilly or remote areas and particularly in the regions of southern India, but this too is mainly confined to the Brahmana community, and even very few among them might be practicing it with the true spirit of the religion and in the real sense of the words. Otherwise it ought to display their pride and vanity and becomes a subject of hypocrisy. Because a larger majority of the Hindus was not enlisted in the above mentioned scheme of life and with the adoption of new education system and new modes of livelihood and the new system of economy, technology etc., the basics of the social obligations are often been ignored and very little concern is visible for keeping the things in order.

As far as the Buddhist and Jain traditions are concerned, there we may find some definite social ethics which an individual is supposed to follow. The observance of the principles of self-restrain and non-violence are the two essential features of most of these communities even today. The adherents of Sikh faith are more known for their service, 'kar seva' to others in their personal capacity.

The Muslims in India alike the followers of Islam everywhere as individuals are expected to observe purity, 'waju', and truthfulness and offer charities, 'jaquat', to the needy peoples as per scriptural rules. And so is the Christian community in India which is supposed to be bound by the ten-commandments in order to maintain personal morality and serving the humanity. But it should also be kept in mind that both the Christianity and Islam are the religions mainly based on community behaviour and apart from general human and moral ethics they do not prescribe any specific rites or rituals to be observed by individuals privately with whatever personal and social motives. The general rule of the gap/difference between the scriptural/religious prescriptions and the actual practices, however, apply to most of the peoples irrespective of the faith they claim to be following.

Shweta Dubey.

Preface

Globalisation has been defined as the process of rapid integration of countries and happening through greater foreign trade and foreign investment. In essence, it refers to increased possibilities for action between and among people in situations irrespective of geographical considerations as per the definition of social theorists. Due to economic liberalisation and globalisation, the world has become a "global village".

There is increasing interaction among people of different countries. As a result food habits, dress habits, lifestyle and views are being internationalised. There has been both positive and negative impact of globalisation on social and cultural values in India. There is no denying of the fact that globalisation has brought cheers to people's life by opening new vistas of employment. It has also made inroads in the cultural heritage of this country.

Every step of movement towards economic, political and cultural modernisation, taken by the state in India, is responded to by the people with an enhanced sense of self-consciousness and awareness of identity. Cultural modernisation, sponsored by the forces of globalisation, is resented if it encroaches upon or does not promote the core cultural values of society, its language, social practices and styles of life. The vigour of the renewed sense of self-awareness generated among the members of the local cultures and communities is such as to succeed in making adaptive reconciliation with the forces of globalisation. The linkages both visible and invisible, defining the cultural interdependence among communities and regions in India which have existed historically, reinforce instead of threatening the national identity. These bonds seem to become stronger as India encounters the forces of modernisation and globalisation.

Prologue

The term 'Globalisation' is in itself self-explanatory. It is a global platform for maintaining evenness in the living mode of the individuals all over the world. Globalisation is the resultant of the interchange of worldly views, opinions and varied aspects of the culture all over the world. This is the method of giving the globalised world a way of intermixing of individuals from various segments, culture and lingos and figure out how to move and approach socially without harming and influencing every others' prestige and glory. Globalisation highly affects social, fiscal, political, and mutual existence of nations. Plentiful hypothetical investigations exhibited that globalisation mediates in a social existence of people that pertains various basic issues.

Globalisation is depicted by scholars as the procedure through which social orders and economies are incorporated through cross-border flows of thoughts, correspondence, innovation, capital, individuals, finances, merchandise, administrations, services and information. The term globalisation means international integration, the world trade prospects being opened, development of advanced means of communication, internationalisation of financial markets, growing importance of MNC's and population migrations. It has also widened the scope of the mobility of persons, goods, capital, data and ideas. It is a way through which the dissimilar world is unified into one society.

The wave of globalisation started entering and effecting India at the end of the last century and still the country is flowing with the present of global changes. Globalisation has both positive and negative effects all through the globe.

May it be business, trade, and work exposure or the economic and financial status of the nation; no field is deserted from the scope of globalisation. The culture and way of living of any nation does not just depict the region and dialect of the locale, yet it also shows with the attitude and mindset of its people. Indian culture is very rich for its legacy and assets, and the warm approach of its residents. India is bunch of flowers consisting of various religion, languages, food, cuisine and edibles, convention, custom, music, craftsmanship and architecture and so forth, packaged into a solitary unit of patriotism and solidarity.

The common factor of these varieties is the Indian attitude of greeting, welcoming, celebrating unitedly with immense friendship and harmony. This is the rich embodiment of the Indian culture that has pulled in numerous non-natives to remain back in India and blend into its interminable fragrance. When we analyze this rich culture with the globalisation perspective, we can discover many inferences of westernisation and blending of different attributes and societies into our delightfully woven cover. As every coin has two sides likewise globalisation also has its positive and negative effects.

CHAPTER ONE

INTRODUCTION

As per the objectives of this book, initially the meaning and nature of globalisation and modernisation will be discussed. Afterwards, its impact on Indian society will be elaborated under separate headings of structural changes pertaining to the social organisation and systems of castes and class, marriage, and family. The changes in the observance of religious rites and rituals will be discussed next. The impact of globalisation and modernisation upon the occupational pursuits and the standard of living will be explained separately besides overall cultural life of the people at the end. All of the above impacts will be briefly summarised under a separate heading.

CHAPTER TWO

OBJECTIVES

- To explain the concept and nature of Globalisation and Modernisation with a view understand its merits and demerits.
- To look into the impact of Globalisation and Modernisation on the Indian social systems and cultural life.
- To make a student able to distinguish and explain the differences between traditional and current patterns of the Indian people in order to clear the confusions arising in the minds of the visitors and making the latter more curious about the country called India.

CHAPTER THREE

OVERVIEW

To understand the meaning of the subject, one must keep in mind that human civilisations and cultures in the remote past developed independently and separately in their isolated regional/geographical settings as per their natural situations.

The human mind has always been interacting and negotiating with its surroundings and developing its belief systems and social practices, so you come to know about various cultures of anteriority. Earlier, the contact between such cultures was meager and confined to some adventurous traders who were able to establish contact with distant areas, for example, you know about trade links even between the proto-historic Indus and its contemporary Mesopotamian civilisations.

With the conquering of the alien regions and peoples by some ambitious leaders and the emergence of vast political empires, however, larger areas were knit together, which also opened the gates of cultural interaction and progress of synthesised cultures and civilisations, expansion of trade links, and so on, in broader areas. Furthermore, with the emergence and progress of new religious movements, Buddhism, Christianity, and Islam in particular, a greater number of people came together under their shades of religious culture, widening the boundaries of humanity.

Thus, humanity, at large, has always been aspiring for expanding and widening the area of its activities in harmony and peace, despite the experiences of conflicts and wars quite contrary to it. The movement of travelers and adventurers from one part of the world to the other in the past and the penning down of their travelogues for posterity was part of the same quest for humanity.

However, now you will know that globalisation, along with modernisation, is quite a new phenomenon, both economic and cultural, in various stages of progress of humanity, which has brought about almost a revolutionary impact on the societies of the world. Indian society, in particular, known to be bound by long traditions on the one hand and variously classified in economic terms on the other, is taking this impact in multiple ways. It refers to changes in social structure, marriage and family systems, new attitudes towards religious rites and practices, new occupational scenarios, changing standards of living, and new cultural patterns.

CHAPTER FOUR

NATURE OF GLOBALISATION

Globalisation has become popular since the last century in the context of international trade regulations. Philosophically, the concept of global humanity developed as early as Vedic times in India. The slogan of 'Vasudheva Kutumbakam' and 'Krinvanto Vishvam Aryam' (Rigveda: IX. 63. 5) were such expressions meaning that 'all the people on the earth are a family' and 'the whole of the world should be Aryanized' (Acculturated) respectively.

Later, religious movements in India and elsewhere also tended to bind the people of the whole world in an ethical knot in their own ways and limitations. However, globalisation of the present age has some specific connotations and a different approach towards making people and cultures of the world come together for the progress of humanity at large. Globalisation is the system of interaction among the countries of the world in order to develop the global economy. Globalisation refers to the integration of economies and societies worldwide. It involves technological, economic, political, and cultural exchanges, made possible largely by advances in communication, transportation, and infrastructure.

While the horrible experiences of the two world wars in the twentieth century had made the world community wise enough to look for such effective organizations at the world level, which could bring about cultural and political harmony among nations, it was further felt that this could not be achieved without economic progress and the uplift of the standard of living of all communities in whichever corners and regions of the world.

Hence, a new approach to fulfilling this objective was conceived and planned. Economic assistance programmes through world agencies such as the World Bank and a Consortium of Funds with the name International Monetary Fund (IMF) for different schemes of development, particularly in developing and underdeveloped nations on the one hand, and the regulation of trade between nations with the specification of items and their quantity and even its production through the World Trade Organization (WTO) became the major planks of this globalisation.

Thus, Globalisation in the modern age does not simply mean the universalisation or spread of any philosophy or ethics for the world community, but it claims to be an economic program intended to minimise the economic disparity among nations and communities.

In practice, however, it intended to devolve upon the developing and underdeveloped nations the responsibility of freeing or cutting down the duties on import of items from other nations, compulsory import of certain items in exchange of their items of export, etc., which is presently termed as the policy of liberalisation. In this sense, globalization is virtually equivalent to economic liberalisation, implying that trade barriers are opened at the national level.

The direct entry of foreign funds and the operation of Multinational Companies in other nations' domains is an important feature of globalisation. This has certainly encouraged the movement of goods and people alike at the global level. It also offers new opportunities in the service sector and the flow of money from one place to another.

The broadening of trade links has furthered social and cultural contacts and has enhanced the standard of living for a class of people who are either managers and administrators, or a part of this system with their befitting skills and expertise. Globalisation, along with modernisation, is penetrating deep into the psyche of the people, particularly of the urban citizenry of countries in the areas of technical and vocational education, health care, sports, leisure, entertainment, and touring. However, the negative implications and impacts of globalisation need to be examined separately.

CHAPTER FIVE

NATURE OF MODERNISATION

When you start talking about modernisation, an immediate thought comes to mind that it is a way of living with modern ideas and institutions as well as new means and technology. Modernisation is often likened to Westernisation, with the assumption that almost all new institutions and technology have been imported or adopted from the West in the modern age.

Noted Sociologist M.N.Srinivas preferred the term 'Westernisation' to modernisation. Milton Singer (Traditional India: Structure and Change, Philadelphia, 1959), Yogendra Singh (Modernisation of Indian Tradition, Jaipur, 1983), and some other sociologists prefer 'modernisation' in place of 'Westernisation'. Srinivas argues that the term" modernisation' is subjective, while the term 'Westernisation' is more objective (Seminar, 88, 1986:2). According to him, the concept of Westernisation refers to "the changes in technology, institutions, ideology and values of a non-western society as a result of cultural contact with the western society for a long period" (Srinivas, Caste in Modern India and Other Essays, Bombay, 1962, p. 55; Social Changes in Modern India, Los Angles, 1966). Further, he suggests that, to some extent, Westernisation has also been complimentary to the process of 'Sanskitisation' (Acculturation) of the lower castes in India with the general access to new technology, democratic institutions and freedom of choice of social and religious rites. Because, Sanskritisation in earlier days happened to be a social mechanism of assimilating various communities and clans into a broader canvas of Brahmanical culture, maintaining at the same time, the ritual distance between the Brahmanas along with other higher castes and the lower castes, but the latter are now trying to catch up with them socially with the new tools of Westernisation in their hands.

Modernisation, however, has a wider meaning and many dimensions. Though it is not a philosophy or movement with a clearly articulated value system, it should be remembered that the modern era was initiated with the renaissance and reformation in Europe and elsewhere, which meant the revival of the spirit of reasoning and rationality. Historically, it implied that humanity had done away with this spirit in the Middle Ages, which was to be corrected with the change in circumstances. The process of change, of course, started appearing in the establishment of new political, administrative, economic, social, educational, technological, military, and so forth institutions. This is perceivable in the behavior of the individual, group, community, or society at large. It is perceivable in terms of food and clothing habits and the standard of living. This is reflected in the changes in social structure, marriage and kinship systems, religious rites, practices, and so on.

CHAPTER SIX

IMPACT OF GLOBALISATION & MODERNISATION ON INDIAN SOCIETY (Part - A)

The impact of Globalisation and Modernisation on Indian society is both apparent and fundamental. It has to be first examined in terms of the changes in the social structure and marriage and family systems, as well as religious attitudes and practices of different shades.

6.1 Social Changes: Structural- Caste, Class, Marriage and Family

At the social structural level, there is a decline in the traditional principle of ascribed status and role to achieve status and role. The castes in India were theoretically and traditionally bracketed with the fourfold division and the hierarchy of the Varnas; Brahmanas, Kshatriyas, Vaishyas, and Shudres, as well as a fifth known as ati-Shudras or untouchables. Since the hierarchy of the castes and discrimination based on this theory has now been totally rejected in the modern democratic constitution of India, new vistas of structural social change have been opened.

The democratic system of achieving political power based on numerical support, affirmative action programs on the part of the government, and special provisions for the uplift of the deprived or low sections of society, modern technology, institutions, new occupations and nature of services, and new means of earning bread and accumulation of wealth, banking system, etc. are various other factors contributing to structural social change pertaining to the caste and class structure of Indian society.

Yogendra Singh believes that a unique feature of modernisation in India is that it is being carried forward through adaptive changes in traditional structures rather than structural dissociation or breakdown. According to

M.N. Srinivas, the occupations practiced by castes, their diet, and the customs they observe, determines their status in the hierarchy. Thus, practicing an occupation such as tanning, butchery, or handling toddy puts the caste in a low position. Eating beef, fish, and mutton is considered defiling. Offering animal sacrifices to deities is viewed as a lower practice than offering fruit and flowers. As such, castes following these customs, diet habits, etc., adopt the life of Brahmanas to achieve a higher status in the caste hierarchy. Though theoretically forbidden, this is the movement of a low caste upward in the social structure of a generation or two. This, in his view, is now also linked to westernisation, which furthers these possibilities.

Another dimension of structural change is the rejection of old values and social conditions. In this context, it may be pointed out that the formation and settlement of castes in earlier times was related to the factors and scope of mobility and non-mobility of occupations and people under the hegemony of traditional priestly and political powers. The castes continued to remain enclosed groups in a self-sustaining closed economy of rural or village settings, and this number increased on the basis of little or more distinctions of occupation, technique, food and dress habits, rites and customs, regions, etc. The urban impact, on the other hand, has always been negative to calcification of castes.

Even if there is no rejection of older values and systems, people tend to move away from them in urban settings. Traditional norms and restrictions on inter-dining and inter-caste marriages among different caste people are rapidly diluting in big cities. Modernisation or Westernisation with globalisation has changed the traditional caste structure with the formation of new social classes. Restriction on inter-dining is almost a thing of the past, even in smaller cities. Inter-caste and even inter-religious marriages no longer invite that wrath on the part of parents and the related community at home if solemnised between capable youths in big cities.

A new class of professionals, administrators, managers, and persons in other service sectors is rapidly emerging with the advent of multinational companies (MNCs), the opening up of new sectors of service, and the establishment of new institutions and organisations such as NGOs. A new compact of people is in the making of their respective organisations based on the equality of their standard of living. This is quite explainable in terms of the faster growth rate of middle classes of different grades in India over the last two to three decades, which is now around 40 percent of the large Indian population.

The impact of Globalisation and Modernisation on institutions of marriage and family are also perceivable particularly in the urban life. Though the marriage rites and general conditions of marriage remain the same as per regional customs even in the cities, but some new ways of celebrating the occasions have come into practice. These are manifest in performance of engagement and marriage ceremonies at different venues, normally hotels or lawns, than at the house of groom or bride. New cuisines go on adding to the throwing of dinner at the occasion.

Sometimes these are organised jointly by both the parties. As far as the practice of dowry is concerned, though it is prohibited by law, it has taken the form of gifts depending upon individual attitude of the parties, as the greed for acquiring more and more resources of living and property by any means has also developed as a result of modernisation. Marriage as a compulsory institution is also being questioned by a few ultra-modern persons for their increasing claims of individual freedom. Even the educated and self-dependent girls in the cities sometimes tend to prefer unmarried life lest their individual personality not be compromised. An extreme position is now being taken in 'live-in-relationship'. Separation and divorce among couples are also becoming more acceptable in the society. It is, however, a matter of debate for the social scientists whether all this should be taken as positive or negative impacts of modernisation.

The family system is also affected. The traditional system of joint families, when at least two to three generations are used to living together in an agricultural or rural setting, is rapidly breaking in urban areas. Since the new nature of occupations and services is taking the people off to distant places within and outside the country away from their native places, and even the persons in the first generation are not able to live together because of their engagement at different places, a general tendency is towards the nuclear family, which means living just the couple and their children until the latter are dependent and not married. The cost of education for the children and the growing standard of living are also pushing such nuclear families to keep away from the joint responsibilities of the families. The urban elite are fast adopting the concept of having only one or two children.

A fallout effect of modernisation may be seen in the tendency of sex detection of the child with the help of new medical techniques before its birth in order to get at least one male child among couples, particularly in cities. This is because a male child in Indian society is considered necessary for the funeral rites of parents. In addition, a female child is looked upon as a burden and a cause and source of insecurity, drawing away from family resources and assets by a number of parents. However, the same attitude towards a daughter or a girl is not met with everyone, and you may find persons or families contrary to this thought cherishing, at the same time, the birth and upbringing of a daughter in their utmost capacity in this modern age.

The above feature of the nuclear family, however, is further depriving future families of many kinds of kinships, as there could be no real brother or sister, daughter and son, sala and sali (wife's brother and sister), jija (sister's husband), bua and phupha (father's sister and her husband) and chacha and chachi (father's brother and his wife), mama and mami (mother's brother and his wife), mausi and mausa (mother's sister and her husband), and the like relations to many persons that have long remained the mainstay of the Indian family system. With the dilution of family bonds and growing self-centeredness, the family structure, particularly in urban India, has been badly affected and seems to be heading towards Western systems of family.

Yet, many traditional customs of families are still prevalent in different regions of the country, and different communities in India have taken the effect of or adopted new ideas, institutions, and technology in a manner suitable to their traditions. Hence, the impact of Globalisation and Modernisation in India varies from community to community and region to region, which is also related to the pace of infiltration of modern systems and urbanisation of the areas.

6.2 Impacts on Religious Rites and Practices

The impact of Globalisation and Modernisation on the religious life of the people in India is worth noting, considering that Indian society is religiously minded. You may find the present religious scenario in India confusing. Apparently, there is a greater tendency to visit religious shrines and temples in the deities.

Numerically, pilgrimage is growing leaps and bound with the facilities of transport and communication, and even many in the younger generation are fascinated to go around for pilgrimage sake. Individual devotees and group processions of Kanvariyas and others can be seen rushing to different religious spots and shrines of saints and gurus during prescribed or popular seasons.

Religious fairs and festivals such as Kumbha melas, Deewali, Dashera, Chhatha Puja, Durga Puja, and Ganesh Mahotsava are now being organized with more gaiety, and an increasing number of people are being assembled on such occasions. Many other religious programs of mass assemblage are also becoming popular with new systems of advertisement, such as electronic and print media. A number of new shrines and temples with gorgeous structures are emerging all around the country, and older sites are being renovated. Then, you see a mushroom growth of new babas and swamis preaching around religious ethics, and some of them even display their magical and mysterious powers and suggest curious means and ways to their followers to get rid of their miseries or fulfilling some of their desires and ambitions.

This may indicate a growing indulgence of the peoples in religious affairs, but sociologically it may be understood as a result of new facilities of transport, communication, and advertisement of the programmes on one side, and a growing sense of insecurity and frustration, stress, and challenges of living and work in the modern age on the other, along with the multiplying population in the country.

Given the above scenario of the religious life of Indian people, it is also important to note the other side of religious practices. Traditionally, a number of religious rites were to be performed by individuals privately as their daily rites or as special rites under the supervision of a priest in Hindus. This practice is now becoming unpopular in big cities with lifestyle changes and the lack of availability of exclusive priests in the vicinity. Moreover, it appears to be difficult to visit a shrine or temple or to join a religious gathering that more often serves other purposes of outing, shopping, etc. than engaging oneself in daily rites and rituals, as well as bothering about ethical commitments of the religion. This can be taken as a practical impact of the new economic systems and urban culture of the modern age.

CHAPTER SEVEN

IMPACT OF GLOBALISATION & MODERNISATION ON INDIAN SOCIETY (Part - B)

The impact of Globalization and Modernization is more visible in the new occupational structure, changing standard of living and new cultural patterns of the peoples in India.

7.1 Occupational Changes

The impact of Globalisation and Modernisation is more visible in the new occupational structure, changing standard of living and new cultural patterns of the people in India.

7.1 Occupational Changes

As modernisation implied revolutionary changes in scientific information and technology, traditional occupational structures were bound to be replaced by new occupations. College trained engineers working in large industrial settings and having higher social status due to their better standard of living with their higher source of income started challenging the existence of traditional artisans and craftsmen with lower social status and lower source of income. Although some technological aid also went into traditional craftsmanship alongside the new demands of the market, which somewhat helped raise the economic status of these artisans and craftsmen for some time, this too appeared to be losing with total automation of the manufacturing of goods in the industrial sector. The traditional guilds of artisans gave way to the industrial groups. There is a demand for trained managers to run the industry.

A new class of administrators as well as the 'babus' (office assistants) for conducting and assisting the work in newly formed institutions and organizations also came into existence both in the public and private sector. A big change was also visible in health sector, where again the college trained medical graduates started taking over the traditional 'vaidya' and 'hakim' with medicines of quick relief and their more organized nursing homes. Education was another sector that experienced sea change in its nature and form of imparting knowledge and training. New types of schools, colleges and universities required new kind of teachers in the place of traditional 'pathashalas' and 'madarsas' run by traditional individual teachers.

The defense organisation of the new nation and the need for the police force to maintain internal law and order also opened avenues for new types of services. A host of other avenues for skilled and non-skilled workers was opened with the building of new infrastructure in the areas of transport, such as roads, railways, waterways, and aviation, and construction of office and institutional buildings and residential colonies in both the public and private sectors.

Changes in occupational structure started occurring even more rapidly with further technological development in space, satellite, and software technology, and revolution in information technology, along with the arrival of multinational companies, particularly with globalisation and liberalisation. Even the basic sectors of production, such as agriculture and base industries, have started experiencing an inflow of professionals with new technological knowhow. Both inland and foreign trade and new business organisations have started looking for personnel with more advanced managerial skills and expertise. There is a demand for professionally qualified persons.

A large number of large industrial groups and public organisations have developed their own Research and Development (R&D) wings to explore the possibilities of enhancing the quality and variety of their products and marketing. Electronics and Computer operations, education and health, hospitality and tourism, food and beverage, sports, and defense are some of the main areas that draw people to cities and organisations offering newer types of occupations. A big thrust is on towards professional and vocational education and training, which has also furthered the establishment of such centers in cities, universities, and colleges, requiring specialized teachers of the trade at the same time. Thus, a new occupational structure is bringing about significant changes in the traditional Indian social system.

7.2 STANDARD OF LIVING

The biggest change as a result of Globalisation and Modernisation can be observed in the standard of living of people. The new technology has tremendously lured people to the exploitation of nature and natural resources to fulfill their needs and avail luxuries. As far as India is concerned, there is a serious problem of space for shelters for all with the swelling population in urban centers. While only a small number of people are capable of affording large bungalows and maintaining their private lawns and gardens, there is a great rush for flats in multistoried buildings, even in smaller cities and cabal towns. Living in a flat and the societies organised for that is itself a new experience for people. Such societies have come up as smaller townships in their right, having all the essential facilities of a market, nursing home or a physician, gym, swimming pools, sports arena, library, club house, etc., in a secure and protected environment.

***Urban Home**: Both Globalisation and Modernisation have provided a new look at the homes of individual families with the availability of a variety of goods and fanciful things in the market, including foreign items. Starting from household furniture, wardrobes, mats, carpets, tiles, television, computer, music and sound systems, refrigerator, bathroom geezers and tubs and sanitary fittings, washing machines, desert coolers, air conditioners, a modular kitchen, tens and hundreds of electronic gadgets and appliances for it, and other utility and luxury items, a modern home may now be found equipped with so many things depending on the resources of income of a person or a family. Keeping one's own means of transport, like two wheelers and cars or vans, even both of it and more if possible, is another addition to this standard of living. Carrying one or more cell phones has also become the order of day, even for those who are unable to afford all the above-mentioned luxuries. 'Live simply and think highly' is no more the ethic of life for the people of this new era.*

***Food Habits**: Despite carrying on their traditional food habits and banking upon their family staple food, a modern Indian family ought to adventure in a variety of new cuisines of different regions, as well as continental. This includes South Indian snacks and Chinese, Italian, and French dishes. Packed and half-ready food materials readily available in the market are a useful source for such experiments at home. Electrical and electronic gadgets such as refrigerators, ovens, microwaves, and mixing appliances have made processing easier. New dining decorations and decorum and the use of fancy cutlery have further added to the gaiety of the feeding habits of urban Indians. A big trend of relishing fast food or junk food on the roadside and going to restaurants and hotels for eating has also developed in the cities.*

Dress Habits: *As far as the dress habits of the Indians in the present are concerned, it has already been changing ever since the rule of Britain in India. It was earlier mainly related to the introduction of new systems of education and work in the colonial period, which, of course, amounted to the Westernisation of Indian systems. Men in the cities quickly adopted the Western styles of trousers, shirts, and coats, whereas the women in India were slow to adopt Western dress, because there was almost no scope for a woman to go for her education and work or to any social place independent of men even in the cities. However, with the growing opportunities for her movement, encouragement of women's education, and growing acceptance of a working woman in the upper castes and middle class of Indian society, there has been a great change in the dressing and clothing of women, at least in the cities. The dresses are not simply confined to Western adoptions, but now it is a global phenomenon and fashions may arrive from any part of the world, suiting the psyche of change and glamour, even for a short time. The dress designers and companies sell their products through large-scale advertisements and fashion shows. So much so that you have now entered the era of designer attire and clothing in large cities.*

Education of Children: *The Children's education has become a big issue for parents today. Although some big efforts are going into reorganizing the public education system and education of children is being made compulsory, due to deterioration and lack of public commitment to the schooling and education of children at the ground level, there is a great desperation in finding good schools for children. Obviously, there is a mushroom growth in schools and colleges in the private sector, which are charging high fees for their maintenance. Parents are likely to send their children to the* *best of such schools and colleges in their vicinity or even to distant places, to some foreign countries like Australia, England, and the U.S. as well, as per their resources, with the objective of making them compete with the demands of the new world. Besides regular schooling, there is also a big trend of sending children to attend coaching classes for some particular standard or for clearing some entrance and competitive examinations. These coaching centers or institutes again demand handsome fees for coaching depending on the reputation of their center, which is affordable by not many. It has also become a status symbol for parents as to what type and level of education they can afford their children. The introduction of computers and the revolutionary growth of information technology are significantly changing modes of learning. Online courses on Internet and websites have offered access to so many new things for students as well as professionals.*

Health Care: *A Considerable attention has been paid to health care in this age of globalisation. Many business agencies and social organisations are out of campaigning for maintaining good health. Public shows of yoga and other exercises and displays of yoga, aerobics, etc., as well as medical counselling on television shows, are all part of this campaign, which, of course, is also a new area of medical business. The affluent class of society is out to keep the apparatus for exercise, such as trade machines, at home. The richer class even has its own private gym and swimming pool. Otherwise, a good number of people of all age groups in big cities tend to join gym, health, yoga clubs, and youths ought to join sports arenas and stadiums, swimming pools, and golf clubs in their vicinity. Big business enterprises and offices are now offering gym facilities to their workers to relax their muscles as a respite from their tidy office work. Walking, running, and laughing* *exercises in the morning and evening have become common features of urban life. Then, you may also find people concerned more about their regular medical check-ups in order to prevent any ailment or to get it cured at the initial level, if detected. There are specialized doctors and nursing homes for general and specific ailments or diseases. Maternity homes are now on the order of the day, and both rich and common people now prefer to use these homes for childbirth and care.*

Market and Malls: *The talk about a new standard of living will be incomplete if you miss the most common feature of shopping in the markets, both in the smaller towns and big cities. It is an age of business and people are lured to buy utility and fashion items all the time. Big departmental stores and showrooms of different products have already made their mark alongside the petty retail shops in the market. A new culture of Mall has developed in big cities that offer fanciful items and entertainment to customers or visitors. A number of big malls are coming up in big cities and even in cabal towns where people flock in for everything fashionable they wish to avail.*

7.3 CULTURAL IMPACTS

In India, people live in both their traditional culture and modern lifestyle. Many new colors have been added to traditional fairs and festivals as a result of globalisation and modernisation. Apart from popularly known festivals of Diwali, Durga Puja and Navaratra, Holi, Lohri, Pongal, Ganeshotsava, Makar Shankranti, Eid, Baquareid, Muharram and Shab-e-Baraat, Guru Nanak Jayanti, Christmas, Ishtar and Goa Carnival, Buddha Purnima and Navaroj, a number of old and new fairs and festivals are celebrated in different states of India all around the year.

To name a few in addition to the above mentioned festivals you may refer to Badri-Kedar festival, Ganga festival, and International Yoga Week at Rishikesh in Uttarakhand; Shiva

Ratri, Ganga Mahotsav, Deva Deepawali, Lolark Chhatha, Buddhava Mangal and Mahamoorkha Sammelan on Ganga ghats at Varanasi, and Buddha Mahotsav at Saranath, and daily Ganga Arti both at Varanasi and Hardwar; Taj Mahotsav at Agra and Avadh or Lucknow Mahotsav, Vrindavan Shardotsav, Hariyali Teej in Haryana; Baba Bakla, Chhapar Mela, Harballah, Sangeet Sammelan and Mukutsar Maghi fair in Punjab; Chait, Flaich or Oo-Khyang, Ghantul festival, Maghi, Phagli, Pauri Yatra, Tushimig, Bala Sundari fair, Chhatrari fair, Dhoogri fair, Gaddi fair and Gugga fair in Himachal Pradesh; Hemis festival, Mansar festival and Mei Lozar in Jammu and Kashmir; Mahamoorkh Sammelan in Chandigarh and Festival of Garden (earlier known as Rose Festival) both at Chandigarh and New Delhi; Mango festival, Phool Waloon ki Sair, International Kite festival and National Day celebrations at New Delhi; Bohag Bihu, Magh Bihu, Kangali Bihu, Ali-Ali Ligno festival, Amsbubashi Mela (Kamakhya shrine) and Tea festival in Assam; Annueno Torgia, Nyokam, Mopin, Tamladu Reh and Boori-Boot in Arunachal Pradesh; Cheiraoba, Chumpha, Ganga-Ngai, Keikru Hitongba, Kut, Lal Haroba, Vaoshang and Ningol Chakouba in Manipur; Behdiengkhlam, Ka Pamblang Nongkrem, Shad Sukmynsiem and Wangala in Meghalaya; Chapchar Kut, Mimkut and Pawl Kut in Mizoram; Amongmong, Aoling, Metemneo, Minakut Moatsu, Monyu, Ngada, Nga-Ngai, Naknyulum, Pikhuchak, Sekrenyi, Tokhu Emong, Tsokum, Tsungremmong and Tulmuni-Yemshe in Nagaland; Pous Sankranti festival, Garia and Gajan Puja, Ashokastami, Kharchi Puja, Orange and Tourism festival in Tripura; Benden Khlam, Drupka Teeshi, Guthor Chaam, Losar, Losoong, Pang Lhausol, Saga Dawa, Shad Suk Mynsiem and Tse-Chuu Chham in Sikkim; Indra Puja, Jhapan, Kali Puja in West Bengal; Dala Chhatha, Malamasa Mela,

Pitrapaksha Tarpan at Gaya, Sonepur Mela (Asia's biggest Cattle fair) in Bihar; Konark Dance Festival, Makar Mela, Magha Mela, Dola or Holi, Taratarini Mela, Chaitra Parba, Rath Yatra, Rajrani Festival, Ashokastami in Orissa; Akhil Bhartiya Kalidas Samaroh at Ujjain, Ameer Khan Festival at Indore, Dhrupad Samaroh at Bhopal and a festival of dance at Khajuraho in Madhya Pradesh; Bhai Dooj, Camel Festival at Jaisalmer, Pushkar Mela at Ajmer and Shilpagram Crafts Mela in Rajasthan; Danga Darbar festival, Modhera Dance Festival, Ambaji Fair, Chitra Vichitra Fair, Shamiaji Fair, Tarnetar Fair and Vasutha no Melo in Gujarat; Banganga festival, Narali Pournima and Vithoba festivals in Maharashtra; International Sea Food Festival, Feast of St. Xavier, Shigmo and International Film Festival in Goa; Ashtabhandhana, Batkamma, Bonalu and Krishna Pushkaram in Andhra Pradesh; Navarasapur-Paltadakkal and Coorg Festival in Karnataka; Mahabalipuram Dance Festival, Chittarai Festival and Ooty Summer Festival in Tamil Nadu; Maquerade and Sani Peyarchi in Puducherry, and Arat Festival, Boat Race and the Great Elephant March in Kerala.

Many of these fairs and festivals are traditionally celebrated earlier than the age of modernisation, but they have gained in stature and dimension due to the ever-growing participation of people with newer items and programs being added to it in their celebration. Besides, you come across a number of secular fairs and festivals have been added to the list, such as Craft Melas, Music and Dance festivals, Mahamoorkh Sammelan (festivals of jest, mockery, and caricature), flower festivals and Feasts and Fates, Book Fairs, Industrial and Agricultural Fairs, and seminars and conferences organized periodically or scheduled as per need and occasions.

Both Classical and folk music and dance traditions are presented in organised stages, and the growing impact of Western music and dance styles is also visible, particularly in big cities with the organisation of big music and dance shows of celebrated Western singers and dancers from outside and within India. Film Festivals also take the limelight due to the ever-widening attraction for films in the new generation. This clearly speaks to the cultural life of the people in present-day India.

Many institutions and organisations have come into existence in the fields of art, music, dance, and drama, such as Sangeet Evam Nritya Academy and Prayag Sangeet Sammelan, which promote the art skills of individuals and groups. Some national-level awards of high repute are offered to people excelling in this field.

Most of the time, people are resigned and confined to their homes after a long and strenuous schedule of their job listening to music, watching television at home, and enjoying home theatres individually or with their family members and friends. Some indulge in their hobbies, such as painting, music, dance, and writing, which are now finding better opportunities for public displays. People tend to go outing to parks or picnic spots on weak ends and Sundays or on holidays. While attending public theatres, musical concerts and dance shows, social and religious discourses, visiting paintings, and art galleries is a cultural feature of the intellectual elite of the city, watching movies in Multiplexes and other cinema halls, and watching big national and international meetings and events like crickets are some of the most common entertainments of the people in the cities. Visiting a Race course and watching car rallies are some specific tastes, whereas attending periodic and occasional public fairs and festivals is the most common feature of the cultural life of the people.

Finally, apart from the growing rush in the traditional pilgrimage discussed above, travel and tour to different sites of historical, cultural, and natural importance and visit and stay at places and sites of sea, hill or water sports, hill stations in summers or winters in addition to the swelling taste of pilgrimages make up most of the cultural activities of the people in the present day. Tourism is gaining importance and efforts are being made, both at the public and private levels, to organize it in a greater way. Travel organisations, agencies, hotels, and tour operators are putting their stakes into the hospitality business and service sector. Companies offer handsome packages to lure people into going around within and outside India.

CHAPTER EIGHT

SUMMARY

Thus, in this book, at the beginning the concept and nature of the two words, Globalisation and Modernisation was explained. While Globalisation in the present sense refers to cross-geographical and cross-national intellectual and economic activities with regard to ideas and knowledge, technology, and services, as well as production, trade, and cultural exchanges and relationships at the global level, modernisation implies change in ideas and attitudes, creation and establishment of new institutions, and change in the standard of living of the people as a whole.

By reading further you could know how the traditional caste structure in India has been affected and a new class of administrators, managers, professionals, etc. has developed in the present Indian society, what new trends have developed with regard to marriage and family systems, and how the families are becoming increasingly nuclear in the urban setting, with an emphasis on individualism, how kinship bonds are affected by the trend of smaller families. Afterwards you could also know about the new scenario of religious life of the people, as you were explained that religious activities in India seem to be expanding in dimension, but individual ethics and private religious rites appear to be declining due to changes in lifestyle.

Globalisation and Modernisation have a significant impact on the upcoming expansion of the service sector with regard to occupations. So, you have found that the occupations are not confincd to certain sectors of production and distribution, but almost an army of professional experts, managers, and office assistants is required to run national and international affairs and business and to serve and cater to the ever-growing needs of society. You have also found that a great change has occurred in the standard of living of the people, particularly in cities with the availability of a host of new articles and appliances and access to new sources of leisure and luxury as per your pocket. The cultural life of people is also changing with the addition of new colors. Better scope and opportunities to showcase and display one's art and individual group aspirations have arisen. All of this makes for the impact of Globalisation and Modernisation has on the Indian society.

The impact of globalisation on Indian societyand culture are as follows:

Family Structure and Role of Women in Family: The joint family which had been the basis of traditional Indian families has undergone serious changes. Those residing in the metropolitan cities in the small flat culture prefer nuclear families. We have lost the persistence to get balanced into the joint family, assimilating the experiences of the older folks and getting the youthful ones raised under the shadow of their grandparents. Kids have begun treating grandparents like visitors or guests, and such upbringing of children is one of the principle reasons of expanding old-age homes, as those youngsters think about their own parents as burden in their adulthood. Although women and men are equal before the law and therefore the trend toward gender equality has been noticeable, women and men still occupy distinct functions in Indian society. Woman's role within the society is usually to perform family and household related activities. However, with the change in time men and women are gaining equal right to education, to earn, and to articulate.

Marriage System and Values: Additionally, marriages in comparison to earlier times have lost their values and morality. It is especially obvious from the expanding number of separation cases and extra-marital affairs reported every now and then. Marriage used to be considered as bonding of souls which will be connected even after the demise of the partners; yet today marriage resembles an expert bond or a purported pledge to share existence without bargaining their self-interests. Traditional ways of arranged marriages by the parents' consent has been replaced by marriage by own liking by the partners. The sense of self factor into the Indian youth is again a result of globalisation.

Infidelity: Both the genders had to maintain a distance as much as possible, with numerous confinements and impediments for a very long time in our culture and way of life. With the rise of globalisation and western culture, youth have begun mixing up well with each other. The cordial approach and the mingling are apparent. The aggregate breakout of restrictions has tainted the Indian mentality, playing up with the physical relationship. A new type of relationship concepts namely live-in-relationship has emerged. Additionally the exaggerated cases of sexual offense cases are the results of the perverted mind that are very much the values considerably alien to our mother culture.

Festivals and Social Values: We have the included values of treating the guests as God, warm-hearted welcoming, greeting elders with due respect and a celebrating every small festival with great colour of enjoyment and togetherness. Such a wide gathering with full shade and light can barely be seen today. Individuals have profoundly limited themselves in social collaboration. The relation in present generation is exceptionally conciliatory thinking about the money related status and riches. We are losing our social morals and ideals and happy moments of harmony and peace. The present age generation is glad observing Valentine's Day and friendship day than Holi and Diwali. Traditionally Namaste, Namaskar or touching of feet of elders is a common way of greeting in the Indian subcontinent. But in modern times 'Hi', 'Hello' is used to greet people in place of Namaskar.

Food, Clothing and Dialect: Indian food, attire and dialects are different in different states. The food varies in its taste having its own nutrient values and each region is specific and rich in its restorative arrangements with the home cures. Indeed, even the attire fluctuates in various states which are especially specific in keeping up the nobility of lady. The various cuisines from different places throughout the world however have distinctive flavours to include; still the food ingredients that have inflicted with much popularity are the junk food items which have increased the health disorders in the country. Again, the dressing like the clothes for the males are an unseemly comfortable for the India n climate. The female dresses are again a diversion to the tainted minds. Indeed, even the Indians are not in favour of promoting their mother tongue or our national language. Rather, the adolescent today view it as a disgraceful condition to talk in their national dialect

Hindi. The manner in which the foreign languages are getting common in India like the French, German and Spanish, right from the school level, gives the examples of the amount of significance we give to Indian dialects and languages in contrast with the remote ones.

Work and Agricultural Sector: India was overwhelmingly an agriculture based nation. With the propelled globalisation and springing up of MNCs, the farming and agriculture has lost its prime importance in India. Agriculture science has minimal concentration among the youths who consider cultivating as a despicable calling. We are losing our wellbeing and our status and gradually getting to the period of financial servitude because of these MNCs.

Education Sector: There are significant effects in academic sector because of globalisation like higher literacy rate and foreign universities collaborating with different Indian universities. The Indian academic system faces challenges of globalisation through info-technology although it offers opportunities to evolve new paradigms shifts in developmental education. Globalisation promotes new tools and techniques such as E-learning, flexible learning, distance education programs and overseas training programs.

Indian Business Culture: The foreign culture has both constructive and contrary impact on individuals and business firms. New ways of thinking and working has developed leading to higher efficiency. Indian organisations have embraced international accounting standards, Just-in-time and other more effective methods of stock control, flextime and new practices of human asset administration, social duty and business morals thoughts, improvement in corporate governance practices, customer relationship management practices, inflow of outside assets and healthy competition with foreign products. The business area in India is profoundly encouraging in the present situation. The effect of globalization has changed the business system in India in terms of psychology, approach, innovation, attitude, work culture and so on.

As a consequence of globalisation Indian industries are adapting themselves to newer challenges and taking benefit from the new and better opportunities making their business all the more profitable with prospects of future growth. The colossal populace of India has made a huge unsaturated market of customers. This is one reason why worldwide organisations are particularly inspired in doing business in India. In the post globalisation period this degree has expanded enormously for worldwide multinational organisations as Government of India has likewise played an exceptionally essential and steady part in this regard through changed liberalised strategies and administrative structure. A few situations that have arisen in India post liberalisation era are as follows: urbanisation and people of rural areas preferring to shift to urban areas, agriculture workers shifting to industry sector, trade market getting opened, boom in international import and export, big open saturated market for products, a growing market for high quality and low price product, gradual increase of organised retail chain, growing range of merger and acquisitions and lucid license policies for overseas multinational corporation. High growth rate is showing economic prosperity in India. Indian market leaders are going global.

Space, Science and Technology: India has created a distinct place in the field of space science and technology viz. launch services, earth observation, communication &

navigation and application of space technology for national development. Today, India stands one amongst the top six space faring nations in the world. The areas that are benefitted/ seemingly to be benefitted with the use of space technology and its applications embrace – resource monitoring, weather forecasting, telecommunication, broadcasting, rural connectivity, health & education, governance, disaster management support, location based services, space commerce together with host of social applications.

Conclusion: India is obtaining a worldwide recognition and slowly moving towards to become a significant economic and political strength. Market economic policies are spreading around the world, with greater privatisation and liberalisation than in earlier decades. Globalisation has resulted in growing global markets in services. People can now execute trade services globally from medical advice to software writing to data processing that could never really be traded before. India features a consumer base of 1.14 billion people. The mobile subscriber base has grown up from 0.3 Million in 1996 to over 250 million currently. In the cities Internet facility is everywhere. Extension of internet facilities has extended even to rural areas. Global food chain /restaurants have already found a large market within the urban areas of India. Lavish multiplex movie halls, big shopping malls and high rise residential buildings are seen in every city. Software Industries and telecommunication sectors are enjoying a tremendous boost in India. Bollywood movies are distributed and accepted worldwide. Programming and software Industries, telecommunications and media segments are getting benefits out of a gigantic lift of this sector in India. Entertainment sector in India has made a significant place for itself in the global market. Indian television channels and serials are watched and liked by people of different countries all over the world. New technologies are being used in agriculture sector resulting in improved yield of crops. Though the development is progressing rapidly, still many basic problems like prevailing poverty in rural areas, menace of corruption and instability of the government in the political arena are a cause of concern and steps should be taken to bring solution to such problems so as to reap the benefits of globalisation in the best possible manner.

CHAPTER NINE

QUESTIONS AND ANSWERS

Question 1: Write about the meaning of Globalisation in the modern age in about thirty words.

Answer: Globalisation in the modern age does not simply mean the universalisation or spread of any philosophy or ethics for the world community, but it claims to be an economic programme intended to minimise the economic disparity among nations and communities.

Question 2: How Globalisation is related to liberalisation of economic practices?

Answer: In practice, Globalisation devolves upon the developing and under developed nations the responsibility of freeing or cutting down the duties on import of items from other nations, compulsory import of certain items in exchange of their items of export etc. which is presently termed as policy of Liberalisation. In this sense Globalisation is virtually meaning economic liberalisation implying thereby opening up of the trade barriers at national level. Direct entry of the foreign funds and operation of Multinational Companies in one another nation's domain is an important feature of Globalisation.

Question 3: Why Modernisation is linked with Westernisation?

Answer: Modernisation is often likened with Westernisation with the assumption that almost all the new institutions and technology have been imported or adopted from west in modern age. Noted Sociologist M.N. Srinivas prefers the term 'Westernisation' to 'Modernisation'. He argues that the term 'Modernisation' is subjective and the term 'Westernisation' is more objective (Seminar, 88, 1986: 2). According to him, the concept of Westernisation refers to "the changes in technology, institutions, ideology and values of a non-western society as a result of cultural contact with the western society for a long period".

Question 4: In what dimensions the process of change in Modernisation is perceivable?

Answer: The process of change, of course, started appearing in the establishment of new institutions in political, administrative, economic, social, educational, technological, military and so forth. It is perceivable in the behaviour of the individual or a group or a community or the societies at large. It is perceivable in food and dress habits and standard of living. It is reflected in the changes in social structure and marriage and kinship systems, religious rites and practices etc.

Question 5: What and how the new class is emerging in Indian society?

Answer: A new class of professionals, administrators, managers and the persons in other service sector is fast emerging with the coming of multinational companies (MNCs) and opening up of new sectors of service and establishment of new institutions and organisations like NGOs. A new compact of peoples is in the making in their respective organisations based on equality of their standard of living.

Question 6: What are the present challenges posed to marriage as an institution in India?

Answer: Marriage as a compulsory institution is being questioned by a few ultra-modern persons for their increasing claims of individual freedom. Even the educated and self-dependent girls in the cities sometimes tend to prefer unmarried life lest their individual personality not be compromised. An extreme position is now being taken in 'live-in-relationship'.

Question 7: What types of kinship the modern nuclear and smaller family units ought to loose?

Answer: The nuclear family and smaller units of modern family is depriving the future families of many kinds of kinships, as there could be no real brother or sister, daughter and son, sala and sali (wife's brother and sister), jija (sister's husband), bua and phupha (father's sister and her husband) and chacha and chachi (father's brother and his wife), mama and mami (mother's brother and his wife), mausi and mausa (mother's sister and her husband) and the like relations to many persons which has long remained a mainstay of Indian family system.

Question 8: What is the new scenario of religious fairs and festivals?

Answer: Religious fairs and festivals like Kumbha melas, Deewali, Chhatha Puja, Durga Puja, Ganeshotsav etc. are now being organized with more gaiety, and more and more number of peoples are assembling at such occasions.

Question 9: How the Hindu society is deviating from the traditional individual religious rites?

Answer: Traditionally a number of religious rites were to be performed by individuals privately as their daily rites or as some special rite under the supervision of a priest in the Hindus. This practice is now becoming unpopular in the big cities with the change in life style and also for the lack of availability of exclusive priests in the vicinity.

Question 10: Who are persons challenging the existence of traditional artisans and craftsmen and how?

Answer: It is the college trained engineers working in big industrial set up and having higher social status due to their better standard of living with higher source of income that have started challenging the existence of traditional artisans and craftsmen having lower social status and lower source of income. Although some technological aid also went into the traditional craftsmanship alongside the new demands of the market which somewhat helped raising the economic status of these artisans and craftsmen for some time, but this too appeared to be losing with total automation of the manufacturing of goods in the industrial sector.

Question 11: What are the factors of rapid occupational changes at present?

Answer: Changes in occupational structure started occurring even more rapidly with further technological development in space, satellite and software technology, and revolution in information technology along with the arrival of multinational companies in particular with globalisation and liberalisation.

Question 12: What are the provisions of residential societies in modern cities?

Answer: Such societies have come up as smaller townships in their own right having all the essential facilities of a market, nursing home or a physician, gym, swimming pools, sports arena, library and club house etc. in a secured and protected environment.

Question 13: What has added to the new tastes in the food habits of Indians?

Answer: A modern Indian family ought to adventure in variety of new cuisines of different regions as well as continental. This includes South Indian snacks, Chinese, Italian and French dishes more commonly. Packed and half ready food materials readily available in the market are handy source of such experiments at home.

Question 14: What is the global phenomenon of clothing?

Answer: The dresses are not simply confined to western adoptions but now it is a global phenomenon, and fashions may arrive from any part of the world suiting the psyche of change and glamour even for a short time. The dress designers and companies are all out to sale their products through big scale advertisement and fashion shows. So much so, that you have now entered the era of designer attires and clothing in the big cities.

Question 15: What is new mode of learning for the students and professionals?

Answer: Introduction of computers and revolutionary growth of information technology is greatly changing mode of learning. On line courses on inter-net and websites have offered access to so many new things for the students as well as professionals.

Question 16: What are the means people commonly adopt for keeping good health in the cities?

Answer: A good number of peoples of all the age group in big cities tend to join some gym or health or yoga club and the youths ought to join sports arenas and stadiums and swimming pools and golf club in their vicinity. Walking and running and laughing exercise in the morning and evening have become a common feature of urban life of the day.

Question 17: What is new feature of organising music and dance shows in present India?

Answer: Both Classical and folk music and dance traditions are presented in organised stage shows and a growing impact of western music and dance styles is also visible particularly in the big cities with the organisation of big music and dance shows of celebrated western singers and dancers from outside and within India.

Question 18: What are the common ways of entertainment of the people in India?

Answer: Watching television at home and movies in Multiplexes and other cinema halls, and watching big national and international meets and events like cricket etc. are some most common entertainments of the people in the cities.

CHAPTER TEN

Reference Books

1. M.N. Srinivas, Caste in Modern India and Other Essays, Bombay, 1962
2. Srinivas, M. N. (1966). Social Change in Modern India. Berkeley, CA: California University Press
3. Milton Singer, Traditional India: Structure and Change, Philadelphia, 1959
4. Yogendra Singh, Modernization of Indian Tradition, Jaipur, 1983
5. S.C.Dubey, Modernization and Its Adaptive Demands of Indian Society, Bombay, 1971
6. M.S.Gore, Education and Modernization in India, Jaipur, 1982
7. A.B.Shah and C.R.M. Rao (eds.), Tradition and Modernity in India, Bombay, 1986
8. Milton Singer, When a Great Tradition Modernizes: An Anthropological Approach to Indian Civilization. Delhi : Vikas Publishing House, 1972
9. The Religion of India (trans. Hans H. Gerth and Don Martindale).Glencoe, Illinois : The Free Press,1960
10. Dr Anshumali Pandey, History of Indian Cookery, 2020.
11. Lotus Arise, Modernization of Indian Tradition, September 12, 2022 https://lotusarise.com/

modernization-of-indian-tradition

CHAPTER ELEVEN

The Author

Presently working as Associate Professor, Human Development, Faculty of Home Science, Banasthali Vidyapith, Rajasthan, **Shweta Dubey** has 24 years' experience of University teaching. She has attended around 50+ International and national seminars, conferences and workshops and has presented 50 paper till now. She has 36 papers and articles published in various International and National Journals, Magazines and Edited books. She has Diploma in Clinical Hypnotherapy from CHI-USA; NLP Diploma and Practitioners from Mind Masters-Trivandrum; Basic training of Gestalt therapy from CAPS -Trivandrum and Certificate of Life Skill Education from Christ University,Bengaluru. She is a trained counselor and Life Coach. She loves to counsel and help people in distress with NLP and Hypnotherapy.

Shweta Dubey was conferred with “Swami Vivekanand National Award 2020”,“Jagatgugu Shri Krisha Samman-2020”. She has received ICONIC FACULTY AWARD 2019 and was conferred with “Swami Vivekananda Excellence Award” 2019, Inquisitive Achiever for Professional 2019 and AWADH SAMMAN SAMAROH in 2018.She was conferred with ANAND - Dr.Pramila Pathak Memorial Award of “Best Counseling Psychologist “2016, Best Paper Award for the manuscript entitled “Enhancing Quality of Teacher Education” contributed to publish in the peer reviewed refereed research journal “INQUISITIVE TEACHER” with ISSN-2348-3717 in Volume I, Issue III December, 2014. She has also got Best Paper Presentation Award on “Developing an Intervention Programme on Physical Changes among Adolescents” by All India Association of Home Science Education (AIAHSE)–IV in 2013.

She is the life member of HSAI, AIAHSE, RSA and some other reputed educational forums and associations. She is also the member of Board of Study and Faculty of Banasthali Vidyapith, Rajasthan and also in the panel of Examiners and Board of Study of some private, state and central universities. She is the member of advisory committee of some reputed schools also. She has designed syllabus for some reputed schools and teacher's training colleges too.

She has been instrumental in International &National workshops, conferences and seminars as coordinator, organizing secretary and organizing committee member. She has been Resource Person for National Conferences, Faculty Development Programmes and workshops and delivered Invited Lectures and also been Panelists at various academic and welfare events.

She has served as NSS officer for 4 years. She is a trained theatre artist herself and was associated with youth festival selection and cooperative committee. She has documented and presented many programs for FM community radio at University level. She has been instrumental in initiating informal education center for villagers also. She has closely worked as co-coordinator for 4 training and welfare projects of UNICEF in Rajasthan. She has developed and implemented intervention programs on reproductive health of women and adolescents, sex education and test anxiety and has also developed a test of creativity for preschoolers. Her major areas of interest are Social and Community Welfare, ECCE, Adolescents and Youth, Guidance and Counseling, Personality Development, Special Education and Elderly, Women and Child health.

Printed by Libri Plureos GmbH in Hamburg,
Germany